McGinty

Y0-CXA-842

WASHINGTON, D.C. IN COLOR

WASHINGTON, D.C.

in Color

A Collection of Color
Photographs by

MARY ELEANOR BROWNING

With Text and
Notes on the Illustrations by

BARBARA NEVILLE STEWART

HASTINGS HOUSE · PUBLISHERS
New York

PUBLISHED 1977 BY HASTINGS HOUSE, PUBLISHERS, INC.
All rights reserved, including the right to reproduce
this book or portions thereof in any form or by any means,
electronic or mechanical, including photocopying,
recording or by any information storage and retrieval system,
without permission in writing from the publishers

Library of Congress Cataloging in Publication Data

Browning, Mary Eleanor.
    Washington, D.C. in color.

    (Profiles of America)
    1. Washington, D.C.—Description—1951–
—Views. I. Stewart, Barbara J. II. Title.
F195.B76   975.3'04   77–13753
ISBN 0-8083-8083-9

Published simultaneously in Canada by
Saunders, of Toronto, Ltd., Don Mills, Ontario

Printed and bound in Hong Kong by Mandarin Publishers Limited

CONTENTS

Growing Pains

WHEN WASHINGTON, D.C., was just a gleam in her founding fathers' eyes, Paris was a somewhat jaded but sill lively lady of nearly fifteen hundred years. London was a sedate matron of over seventeen hundred, and Rome was grand matriarch approaching her twenty-sixth century of existence.

Now that Washington has weathered a stormy adolescence and is coming of age, acclaimed the "loveliest of capitals" and "city of magnificent distances", it shows evidence of its turbulent childhood. A slow-to-develop infant born of quarrelsome parents, raised in poverty in a disease-ridden swamp according to some, alternately spoiled and rejected, gravely injured in a great war and emotionally scarred by later conflicts, the trauma of its early struggles were further complicated by the duality of its political, social, cultural and economic problems.

The roots of this schizophrenia go back even before 1790 when George Washington chose the site for the Federal City. Perhaps it began when the first white settlers sailed up the Potomac. Originally "Patawomeke", Algonquian for "trading place", the river had provided sustenance and transportation for neighboring Indian tribes for at least five thousand years when Captain John Smith first sailed through Chesapeake Bay and up the river as far as Great Falls in 1608. Within a fairly short time of the new settlers' arrival two-thirds of the 20,000 natives were wiped out by white man's disease, liquor or invasion of territory. They left a legacy of place-names you could skip rope to: Accokeek, Accotink and Chicamacomico; Chesapeake, Catoctin, Monocacy and Quantico; Pokomoke, Pamonkey, Piscataway and Tuckahoe.

Virginia at that time included the original Charter granted by King James I to the Virginia Company in 1609, extending 200 miles north and south of Old Point Comfort (near the present Chesapeake Bay Bridge tunnel) from Atlantic to Pacific. She lost her territory north of the Potomac when King Charles I gave Cecil Calvert (Lord Baltimore) a royal grant for a new-world colony in 1631. Calvert named it "Maryland" in honor of Charles' wife, Queen Mary, and sent his brother, Leonard Calvert, in the sailing ships *Ark* and *Dove* to establish the first settlement in 1634.

Arriving in late winter, they settled near the mouth of the Potomac, having purchased thirty miles of land from the Indians in exchange for tools and cloth. The settlement, named "St. Mary's Cittie", prospered from the first, and though it fell into ruin after the government moved to Annapolis in 1695, from this beginning enormous plantations of a thousand and more acres spread up the river. Here began the indenture system that led to the extensive use of negro slaves.

Difficult times had put many men out of work in England, while America was experiencing a labor shortage. Unable to afford the passage to the land of promise, a man or woman (often in their teens) pledged to work from two to five years in return for the fare. A 50-acre head-right entitled a landowner to fifty acres of land for each person he brought to this country. The more land he owned, the more laborers he required, but he kept losing his indentured laborers when their time of servitude expired. Eventually the plantations turned to negro slaves who remained the property of their masters. Within a few years the largest segment of the population was black.

"Sot-weed", as King James referred to the leaf-crop introduced in Virginia by John Rolfe, became the basis of American economy. Travellers carried pouches of tobacco much as the forty-niners were later to carry gold nuggets to pay expenses. Certificates representing tobacco stored in warehouses awaiting inspection, weighing and taxing by British officials before being shipped became legal tender.

British taxes and restrictions on tobacco became a plague that spread to other areas of colonial life with laws that infuriated the colonists, beginning with the British decision to keep a standing army in America in 1763. Each year some new indignity was added, inexorably driving the colonies toward war.

During the Revolution the states were governed by the Continental Congress, first meeting in Philadelphia in 1774. Congress played musical chairs, moving the seat of government from Philadelphia to New York, Baltimore, Lancaster, York, Annapolis, Princeton and Trenton, first fleeing the British and then dodging Continental troops demanding their overdue pay.

All agreed it was time to settle down and choose a permanent site for the Federal City, but the task was complicated by the issue of slavery. Philadelphia, the largest and most civilized American city, seemed the logical choice but slave-owning Southerners opposed the idea because the Quakers were firm Abolitionists. Northerners, on the other hand, objected to establishing the Congress in a slave-holding area because it might appear that the United States Government supported the principle of slavery.

In 1789 the new Federal government began functioning, and unanimously elected George Washington as President. He appointed Thomas Jefferson

Secretary of State, and Alexander Hamilton Treasurer of the United States. These two men of such different backgrounds and persuasions managed to work out a compromise whereby the government was to assume war debts amounting to some $200,000,000 accumulated by the individual states—mostly those in the North—in exchange for Northern acceptance of a Southern capital. The compromise also stipulated that Congress would meet in Philadelphia for a period of ten years while a new seat of government was being built somewhere on the Potomac River. However, strong efforts to move the capital elsewhere continued for years, and not until after the Civil War did the present location of the city receive full acceptance.

President Washington inspected many sites along the Potomac and in 1791 chose an area of Maryland including Georgetown and a section of Virginia encompassing Alexandria. He was well acquainted with the latter town, having surveyed it and purchased two of the original lots. His decision was based on the potential for commerce and industry inherent in that location. Colonel George Mason's hand-operated ferry was doing a brisk business at the point where the main road from North to South crossed the Potomac here. Ocean-going ships could navigate as far as the falls upriver, and from that point a new canal was planned to bring produce from the rich farmland, and iron, coal and lumber from the forests of Ohio. Here, he was convinced, a thriving manufacturing center would develop, and the world would come to trade. And tension between North and South would be eased when new employment opportunities would eliminate the slavery issue in Virginia and Maryland.

Washington's next step set the stage for the first conflict-of-interest situation in the capital when he appointed a three-man commission to choose sites for government buildings and direct the construction of the new city. Unfortunately, all those chosen—Daniel Carroll, Thomas Johnson and David Stuart—had land interests or relatives with large land-holdings in the District. The drama that unfolded included greed, graft, bankruptcy, romance and heartbreak.

The First Act began with the arrival of Pierre Charles L'Enfant, footsore and bedraggled, in 1791. A French engineer who had served with distinction under Washington during the Revolution, he had written the General begging to be allowed to have a part in creating the new seat of government of his adopted country. His carriage had broken down on the journey from New York so he rode horseback and walked part of the distance in a miserable drizzle. Later he wrote "...an heavy rain and thick mist, which has been incessant ever since my arrival here, does put an insuperable obstacle to my wish of proceeding immediately to the survey."

Another surveyor, Andrew Ellicott, had already been on the job for a month, and with the help of Benjamin Banneker, a self-taught black mathematician, surveyor and astronomer of remarkable ability, the District of Columbia was laid out in a ten-mile square with corners exactly oriented on the points of the compass. They marked the boundaries with stones a mile apart, and by using celestial calculations they determined the exact center, and there, on Jenkin's Hill, L'Enfant situated the Capitol Building. Then, a mile and a half away, he placed the "President's Palace". L'Enfant's vision for the capital was colored by his admiration of Versailles.

Between the White House and the Capitol he extended a broad highway, which was named Pennsylvania Avenue, reportedly to ease that state's disappointment in not being chosen for the Nation's Capital. Instead of today's Mall, the architect designed a 400-foot wide "public walk", lined with gardens and lawns leading up to spacious homes. Pretty little Goose Creek, sometimes called the Tiber River, he converted to a canal to be linked with the C. & O. Canal, with a lagoon and wharves near the present Seventeenth Street. A lock-keeper's house still exists at Seventeenth and Constitution Avenue, but the canal was covered over in 1871 after it became a dumping ground for trash and sewage.

Maryland and Virginia had agreed to give the government the land needed, and to provide $120,000 and $70,000 respectively for public buildings, but the remainder of the financing was to come from the sale of lots within the District. Washington persuaded local landowners to sell the land required for the city for around $65 per acre. All acreage remaining after construction of public buildings was to be cut up into small lots and sold, with half the preceeds to go to the government; there was to be no payment for land required for roads. Since the price was many times what the land was worth as farmland, the owners were delighted with their bargain until they found out that the "crazy" architect had designed highways up to 400 feet in width; a total of 3606 out of 6,111 acres was required for streets alone.

The Second Act of our drama begins with the Commission's request that L'Enfant name the streets "alphabetically one way, and numerically the other, the former divided into north and south letters, the latter into east and west numbers", which works as well now as it did in 1791. But he incurred their wrath when he refused to provide a copy of his plan to be used in the sale of lots, fearing this might encourage speculators to monopolize favored areas and unbalance his carefully planned scheme. The sale fell short of expectations and the architect was held responsible.

Within a few months L'Enfant became involved in another controversy with the commission that resulted in his dismissal. He discovered a house under construction exactly where his plan indicated New Jersey Avenue was to be located. Since he had failed to provide the commissioners with copies of his plan it could hardly have been avoided, but although the house was well along, L'Enfant ordered the workmen to remove it. The owner, Daniel Carroll of Duddington, a nephew of the commissioner and the largest landowner in the District, obtained a restraining order. L'Enfant returned after dark and levelled the building.

His firing precipitated a long, bitter struggle between architect and government. L'Enfant billed the government for $95,000, but was paid only $1,394.20. It is ironic that he lived the last years of his life as a pauper at the home of the daughter of Daniel Carroll of Duddington, and was buried in an unmarked grave on the estate near Bladensburg.

The third and final act began after the city had been in limbo for nearly two years after L'Enfant's dismissal. To spark interest in the capital a gala celebration was planned for September 18, 1793 featuring the laying of the cornerstone for the Capitol Building by George Washington himself, followed by a sale of lots. Although the President bought four, the public remained apathetic. Then L'Enfant's prediction regarding speculators began to prove accurate. A wealthy Bostonian, James Greenleaf, formed a partnership with the former Superintendent of Finance, Robert Morris, to acquire 6,000 lots at $80 each, with no money down and no interest! Another heavy investor, Thomas Law, newly arrived from England, met and married Martha Washington's grand-daughter, Eliza Parke Custis, while speculating in real estate in his adopted land.

These entrepreneurs placed such exorbitant prices on the properties that sales halted altogether. Morris had a already secretly invested in other parcels, and when he failed to negotiate the foreign loan he had counted on he was judged to be over thirty million dollars in debt, and both he and Greenleaf spent time in debtor's prison. Thomas Laws' marriage failed, and he, too became a pauper. Apparently it was partly due to Pierre L'Enfant that Morris went bankrupt. The financier had hired L'Enfant to design a mansion for him after the architect was dismissed by the government. The cost of construction ran 1,000 percent over estimates. The house was never finished and L'Enfant never received his $9,000 fee. The epilogue to our drama will take place over 100 years later in 1908.

Meanwhile, the city was in danger of expiring at the tender age of five years. The commissioners realized that drastic measure were needed if the city were to survive. Reluctantly they borrowed $100,000 from Maryland, and Congress appropriated a similar sum. Public confidence rose, and considerable private building took place before George Washington completed his second term in 1796. He died less than six months before his successor, President John Adams, ordered the government moved from Philadelphia to the new capital in accordance with the timetable established by the Constitutional Convention ten years previous.

The entire complement of U.S. Government employees, 126 strong, left the most civilized city in the country for the near-wilderness of Washington. The bankruptcy of land speculators had left deserted, unkempt houses despoiling the land. There was only one tavern, and the nearest accomodations were in Georgetown, a long, rough journey from the Capitol. The Post Office moved into three partly-furnished rooms of a rented building while the Postmaster General's family lived on the third floor. The Senate wing of the Capitol was under roof, and the first departmental building, the Treasury, was under construction.

The exterior of the White House was finished, but the grounds were littered with debris. Inside, only a few of the thirty rooms were habitable. Abigail Adams was 56 years old and in poor health. In her letters of that time, the President's Lady complained of the difficulty of obtaining firewood to heat the damp, drafty rooms, of having no bells to summon servants or announce visitors, and of having to hang laundry in the house.

The Adams spent only six months in the White House, and it was still incomplete when Thomas Jefferson was inaugurated. The Washington skyline during Jefferson's era displayed, besides the Capitol, Treasury and Post Office-Patent Building, the nucleus of Georgetown University and a number of elegant town homes including Octagon House, within sight of the Executive Mansion. Several churches were completed, as were major military installations including the Marine Barracks and Commandant's House, and the Navy Yard on "M" Street along the Anacostia River. But events would soon take place that would set back Washington's progress toward becoming a real city by many years.

Great Britain and France had been engaged in a long and costly war for sixteen years when James Madison took office after Jefferson's second term. The United States had been struggling to stay neutral but increasing restrictions on trade through blockades by both the French and the British had a disastrous effect on American shipping. Finally in 1812 the Senate voted by a narrow margin to engage in a war that should never have taken place. Two days earlier the British Foreign Minister had agreed to repeal the orders that authorized the blockade responsible for the dispute, but the war was underway before the message arrived by courier, and there was no turning back. Better communication would also have prevented the greatest battle of the war, fought at New Orleans *after* a peace treaty had been signed.

But the War of 1812 did take place. It lasted for almost three years, and was fought from Canada to New Orleans, centering in on Washington in 1814. At that time the District had a population of around 6,000 and was operating under the Charter of 1802 providing for a mayor appointed by the president, and twelve elected council members. A dozen government buildings had been completed, and there were houses and taverns scattered along the unpaved streets.

Admiral Sir George Cockburn decided to attack the capital by its back door, bringing British troops through the Chesapeake Bay and up the Patuxent River to Benedict, Maryland. They disembarked and marched for five days without incident until a small, poorly prepared force of Americans met them just outside Bladensburg. After a half-hour battle in which 64 British and 26 Americans died, the Americans retreated to Georgetown. The defenseless Cabinet and President and Mrs. Madison fled into Virginia to watch the smoke billow from the besieged city as the British burned the Capitol, the White House, the War Department Buildings and all other public buildings except the combined Post Office and Patent Building.

Providentially, a fierce wind and thunderstorm battered the capital the next day, and the invaders withdrew, fearing their ships might be sunk by the storm. Later they attacked Baltimore, where both the British Army and Navy were driven back, and the British Government announced it was ready to discuss terms of peace. Under the terms of the treaty negotiated in Octagon House, everything was to be exactly as it was before the war. So an unpopular war that should never have been fought settled no arguments, changed no boundaries, and made little impression on history, but it destroyed the city of Washington.

Only a burnt-out shell remained of the White House, so the President and Mrs. Madison took up residence in Octagon House. James Madison was 5'4" tall while Dolley, at 5'9", wore high heels and towering turbans to emphasize her regal height. Washington Irving wrote of this Mutt-and-Jeff couple, "Mrs. Madison is a fine portly buxom dame who has a smile for everyone...but as to Jimmy Madison, he is but a withered little apple-John." Nevertheless, Madison's second term is known as the "era of good feeling", a time of national growth and prosperity, particularly in the North. It was in this period that Congress granted Washingtonians the right to elect their own mayor and legislators, a system that lasted fifty years.

During the European Wars of 1792 to 1815 the trickle of immigration into the United States became a flood; from an average of 4,000 a year before 1800 it increased to 20,000 in 1818, mostly from England. Between 1815 and 1845 over a million Irish arrived, driven out by the potato famine. Since nine out of ten immigrants went to the North, the South changed more slowly. Southern economy continued to depend on agriculture tended by slaves; the Northerners took Southern cotton, sugar and furs and shipped back manufactured goods, adding freight charges, insurance and the middleman's profit. Planters complained they were sliding deeper into debt with every shipment. So while the North progressed, the South stood still, and the slave controversy still rankled. By 1850 relations between the two were critical.

The District of Columbia had long served as a major outlet for slave ships and overland slave caravans. What is now Potomac Park was the setting for slave pens, and regular auctions were held there. In 1830 there were approximately the same number of free negroes as slaves in the District. By 1860 the relationship had changed to 11,000 free blacks and just over 3,000 slaves. Fearful whites passed stringent laws forbidding blacks to meet other than for fraternal or religious purposes. Even black preachers were outlawed after Nat Turner's insurrection in 1831, and a 10 p.m. curfew was imposed.

California's request in 1849 to be admitted to the Union with a constitution forbidding slavery outraged the Southern states, who claimed the right to take slaves into California. Threatening to secede from the Union, they also demanded that the Northern states stop agitating the slave question, and arrest and return fugitive slaves. The Compromise of 1850 permitted new states to decide whether to be slave or free, but did require the return of escaped slaves. The Fugitive Slave Law was impossible to enforce, and the peace lasted only ten years.

Slavery and economics were the issues of the presidential compaign of 1860, with North and South at opposite poles on all questions. Abraham Lincoln, nominated by the Republicans, favored abolition, tariff laws favorable to manufacturers, and free homesteads for farmers and workers, all repugnant to the South. Following Lincoln's election South Carolina was the first state to secede, and six others had followed suit by the time of Lincoln's inauguration.

Washington became a divided city; both North and South wanted to retain it for their capital. Troops of both sides marched and drilled in the streets. The Confederate attack on Fort Sumter, South Carolina, in the face of President Lincoln's avowed promise to hold Federal installations in the South, precipitated the calling up of the Northern troops.

First to arrive in Washington were the Pennsylvanians. Carrying pitifully few weapons, and dressed in overalls and farm clohes, they were stoned and spat upon as they straggled through Baltimore. Then the New York Regiment arrived by sea through Annapolis. In his book "Abraham Lincoln: A History" John Hay said, "The presence of this single regiment seemed to tip the scales of fate." Without it Washington might have become the Confederate capital, perhaps altering the outcome of the war.

Washington was dreary, desolate and dirty during the four years of conflict, with forts on every hill. Parks and squares became tent cities, and troops were quartered even in the White House. Army wagons and ambulances rolled through the city day and night, with hospital cots for the wounded and dying crowded into churches. Streets swarmed with negro refugees fleeing from slave states, as slavery was abolished in the District in 1862, and the President authorized the enlistment of blacks in the Army.

In 1864 the Confederate Forces under General Jubal Early crossed the

Potomac 80 miles above Washington. After a wide flanking march they suddenly appeared at Silver Spring, Maryland, only six miles from the Capitol. For reasons unknown they failed to take advantage of their position, and their delay in pressing on gave General Grant time to bring in reinforcements and save the capital from another purge of fire.

Only five days after the Civil War ended President Lincoln was assassinated in Ford's Theater on 10th Street, N.W. Now completely restored and furnished, the theater is open to visitors as is the house across the street once owned by William Petersen, a tailor, where Lincoln was carried, mortally wounded.

According to Claude J.Bowers, author of "The Tragic Era", "The twelve tragic years that followed the death of Lincoln were years of revolutionary turmoil. Never have men in responsible positions directing the destiny of the Nation been so brutal, hypocritical and corrupt." Scandals and graft dominated the capital, and the city itself, after the debris of war was removed, was alternately a muddy morass or a hot, dust-driven hell of stinking sewage and rotting huts. Unskilled workers sat in enforced idleness; babies died of disease and starvation, and crime was the only thing that thrived in the atmosphere of poverty and ignorance in the poorer, black neighborhoods.

Yet this was what Webster describes as the "Gilded Age—the period in the U.S. from about 1870 to 1898, characterized by a greatly expanding economy and the emergence of plutocratic influences in government and in the social structure." To illustrate this, an 1882 newspaper article estimated the combined net worth of seventeen senators at about $600,000,000!

The capital was like a beautiful woman with a dirty face, wearing an ermine coat over filthy rags, malnourished and barefoot. But her benefactor was on the way. In 1871 Congress approved a territorial form of government for the District of Columbia, with a governor, a board of public works and a Council of eleven members, all appointed by the president, and a lower legislative body of 22 members and a voteless delegate to Congress elected by the District. President Grant appointed banker Henry Cooke as governor and a local builder, Alexander Shepherd, as a member of the board. Shepherd became chairman of the board and promptly launched an improvement program that scrubbed Washington's face and cured some long-standing ailments such as the road, sidewalk and sewer systems. He tore down disgraceful old buildings, ripped out railroad tracks, put in street lights and improved water facilities. Taxpayers sat up and took notice when he extended roads even beyond the city limits, and demanded his ouster from office when he started planting trees along the avenues. Congress had great faith in Shepherd, however, and when the panic of 1873 drove Cooke out of office Shepherd was appointed Governor.

The depression deepened and the public pressed for an accounting of

Shepherd's spending. In June of 1874 Congress abolished the office of Governor, replacing the three-year old territorial system with a temporary form of commission rule. The investigation that followed placed the city's debt at 22 million, more than twice the ceiling originally imposed. Though he was ultimately cleared of wrong-doing, Shepherd was denied re-appointment as commissioner, and he spent nearly 20 years in exile in Mexico. Upon his return in 1897 the outrage had died down and the importance of his contribution in bringing the long over-due improvements to the city was recognized. A statue erected in a park adjoining the District Building depicts Alexander Shepherd with blue-prints in hand, and he was hailed as the "Maker of Washington", in spite of the fact that the enormous debt he left the city was eventually financed over a period of 50 years, with the final payment not made until 1922.

In 1878 Congress again reorganized the District Government, placing it under three commissioners appointed by the President. This commission in turn was made responsible to congressional committees in order to keep the budget under control after Shepherd's extravagance.

In 1901 President McKinley's assassination elevated to office the first strong president since Abraham Lincoln. Theodore Roosevelt, the youngest president ever to hold the office, brought new excitement and imagination to the White House. With six exuberant children, he or his family made headlines daily. There was nothing he feared to tackle—the railroad industry, coal mine operators, financiers, or foreign diplomats. The Panama Canal was started under his administration. He expanded the Monroe Doctrine to new dimensions. But the grandest contribution to the Washington scene during the Roosevelt era was through the work of the McMillan Commission, a four-man body sponsored by Michigan Senator James McMillan, Chairman of the Senate District Committee, to consider how the city's park system could be improved and the city made more beautiful. The men appointed were highly distinguished in their fields, uncorruptible and generous—they received no salary. Their names were well known to the public: Daniel Burnham, who directed the design of the World's Columbian Exposition in Chicago; Charles McKim, outstanding architect; Augustus St. Gaudens, noted American sculptor, and Frederick Olmstead, son of the landscape architect who laid out Central Park in New York.

First they toured Europe's finest cities. Then, after a year of study, they brought to the District the McMillan Plan, in 1902. This report advocated stripping away the nineteenth-century muddle that had been allowed to accumulate. Their primary finding: "The original plan of the City of Washington, having stood the test of a century, has met with approval. The departures from that plan are to be regretted, and wherever possible, remedied."

Their recommendations saved the mall by cancelling proposed construction of a huge new depot, moving it to Massachusetts Avenue, and tunneling under Capitol Hill to hide the unsightly railroad tracks. They proposed clearing the banks of Rock Creek of years of accumulated rubbish and laying a ribbon of parkway linking Potomac and Rock Greek Parks. They recommended landscaped parkways on both sides of the Potomac River to Great Falls on the north, and south to Mount Vernon (now the serene and lovely George Washington Parkway), and small parks scattered throughout the city. Another major change was the reclaiming of swamps by extending the Mall westward as the site for a new monument for Abraham Lincoln.

They urged that museums and public galleries should line the mall on both sides of the Smithsonian. Buildings to house the legislative and judicial branches of the government were to face the Capitol grounds. Statues, fountains, reflecting pools, ballfields, and "...ample facilities for boating, wading and swimming in summer as well as for skating in winter"—a banquet of delights for all appetites.

The attention focused on the original plan for the city brought new appreciation for the genius who conceived it. The coffin of Pierre Charles L'Enfant was rescued from obscurity and moved to a prominent location in Arlington Cemetery, overlooking the city he designed, providing a happy ending to the drama begun in 1789.

The first allocations appropriated by Congress were for buildings rather than parks. These financed completion of six new buildings by 1908—the District Building, Offices for the House and Senate, the Department of Agriculture, a new National Museum, the Army War College, and the District Public Library. A later appropriation of $600,000 for new parks as a result of the McMillan Plan brought cries of outrage over its unfairness to poor neighborhoods on alleys where as many as a dozen persons lived in a single room with a leaky roof, broken windows and an outdoor privy. Social reformers in the District badgered Congress to improve housing conditions and provide adequate schools and hospitals, but not until Jacob Riis, newspaperman and social worker of national renown, testified before Congress that conditions were worse in Washington than in the grimiest slum in New York was legislation started to combat the problem.

Demolition of some of the worst hovels resulted from the new laws of 1906, but a year later the act was declared unconstitutional and work came to a halt. Attention had been focused on the situation, however, and it became fashionable for women's clubs and debutantes to do good works in the inner city. A "clean-up week" resulted in the collection of 33 wagon-loads of trash from a single block.

Social betterment became a campaign issue in the election of 1912, and the first Mrs. Woodrow Wilson toured the city's alleys and settlement houses. On the last morning of her life in 1914 she told President Wilson that she could rest easier if she knew that the new Alley Bill, proposed in 1913, had passed. It became law in 1819, and forbade residence in any alley not converted to a minor street. Unfortunately, it lacked teeth, and the demand for housing in the war-time capital soon made it meaningless.

From 1917, when the United States entered World War I, until the Armistice in 1918, Washington was the center of activity for the Allied Nations. Soldiers again marched down Pennsylvania Avenue. Men and women came from small towns and farms all over the country to work at the business of war. Temporary buildings were hastily erected to provide office space and housing, some of which remained as eyesores in the capital as late as 1973.

The gates to the White House, closed before the U.S. had entered the war, remained shut as President Wilson's illness brought activities in the capital to a halt soon after the first exuberance of the Armistice had worn off. A pall settled over the city, lasting until the new president took office. Warren G. Harding and his wife opened White House to the sunshine and to the public again, inviting as many as three thousand guests to garden parties.

Business at the capital concentrated on shaping the aftermath of the Armistice, particularly the Disarmament Conference of 1921, until the Teapot Dome scandal erupted. Harding died in office; some said he died of a broken heart, but the official cause was pneumonia.

During the 1920's both private and government building reached an all-time high, spurred by a population boom that reached almost 500,000 in the District. The great Public Buildings Program of 1926, for which Congress made $400,000,000 available, was planned to conform to the L'Enfant and McMillan Plans. Demolition of an encrustation of old buildings on 15th Street near Pennsylvania and Constitution Avenues permitted the redevelopment of the heart of the old commercial city into the last stand of centralized government, the Federal Triangle.

On about 70 acres east of the Ellipse, in a perfect right triangle except that "D" Street cuts off the Northwest corner, were crammed the principal administrative departments of the government. These include—take a deep breath—the Federal Trade Commission, National Archives, Department of Justice, the FBI, Internal Revenue, the old Post Office, the *New* Post Office (built in 1934), Labor and Interstate Commerce, the Commerce Department Building with the Aquarium in the basement, and the United States Information Agency.

The buildings alone cost 78 million and house 30,000 employees. A parking lot for all those employees had to be shoved in between the District Building and the Labor Department, and the resulting volume of traffic created problems that have yet to be solved.

The Federal building program has since snubbed the Triangle area and chosen sites removed from the grossly overpowering structures. The Census Bureau settled at Suitland, Maryland, the Naval Hospital and National Institutes of Health at Bethesda, and the mammoth Pentagon flumped down across the river where her parking lots could flow over the Virginia countryside with space for over 10,000 cars.

Major construction other than government buildings added to the Washington cityscape in recent years includes the Kennedy Center, the Hirshhorn Museum and the National Air and Space Museum, all of which counteract Frank Lloyd Wright's ascerbic observation in 1939 that the buildings of Washington are "...without exception superficially, expensively, falsely traditional."

Democracies tend to mediocrity in buildings, to select architects who design safe, unspectacular works. Neither Wright nor Louis Sullivan, pioneer of the American school of functional design, was ever commissioned to design a building for the Federal Government. Lewis Mumford, in *The City in History*, says "There is no question as to what happened in Washington. L'Enfant's bold conception was brutally massacred; and as if that were not sufficient, it was, in time, visually disrupted and defiled by a wide scattering of unkempt and irrelevant buildings." But the bare bones of L'Enfant's plan remain to guide and inspire future generations; although his part in the drama of the birth of the Federal City lasted only a year, his talent, earnestness and *rightness* for the part are undeniable. And Washington's appeal lies less in its architecture than in the serene beauty of its setting, and in the spirit of its people.

Coming of Age

Picture the District of Columbia as an oversized patchwork quilt 200 years in the making and not yet complete. At a scale of one foot to the mile it would be ten feet square. Now turn it at an angle so the corners are precisely oriented to the North, South, East and West as Banneker and Ellicott laid out the Federal City in 1791.

The quilt is pieced predominately in various shades of green velvet, representing acres of trees and grass in parkland and Mall, The vivid streaks of blue (a *muddy* blue would have been closer to the tuth) are the Potomac and Anacostia Rivers, Rock Creek, the C & O Canal, and the Tidal Basin, with pink silk for the cherry trees lining its banks. Government buildings are done in off-white, pink or gray linen, with the exception of the castellated Smithsonian Institution, which is brick-red flannel. The rectangles of banker's gray worsted are parking lots. Strips of black cambric, sewn in clusters throughout the district but particularly common in the Northeast, are run-down apartments owned by absentee landlords. At 14th Street near Florida Avenue the faded, worn fabric is ripped and charred, though a makeshift attempt has been made to cover it with a hastily-sewn patch. This is the area where burnt-out, boarded-up buildings still offer mute evidence of the bloody rioting that erupted in April, 1968 after Dr. Martin Luther King's tragic assassination.

The whole is quilted in a spider-web of stitches indicating the intricate grid of streets, with embroidered circles or squares at the intersections where avenues pierce the streets. Yarn ties it all together in the locations where over five hundred statues and monuments are located, memorials to heroes claimed by Washington though most of their deeds of glory were performed in places like France, Philadelphia, or Dublin.

Now take a pair of sharp shears and cut along the Virginia side of the Potomac River, removing nearly a third of the quilt's area. This represents the land that retrocessed to Virginia in 1846. Alexandria had felt like a step-child of the District from the moment it discovered that the Constitutional Convention had included a provision in the Charter for the Federal City that all government buildings were to be constructed *north* of the Potomac.

Although it was at one time the third greatest shipping port in the new world, Alexandria declined gradually after George Washington's death. Visiting ships brought in diseases from all over the world, and epidemics of cholera and yellow fever took the lives of many Alexandrians. Disastrous fires occured in 1810 and 1824, destroying major portions of the town. When the C & O Canal was started Alexandria believed it would make a dramatic rebirth, and expected to fare even better under Virginia's jurisdiction. Congress agreed to release all of the District south of the river, but the railroad was completed before the canal and carried most of the freight. Alexandria's docks and wharves were deserted as shipping came to a halt during the Civil War, and the town never recovered its former prosperity. Townspeople felt betrayed and frustrated for generations.

Thomas B. Simmons, city planner, architect and President of the Capitol Hill Restoration Society, says there are two communities within the nation's capital. "One is truly national, with the obligatory concern for the size, scope and functioning of Congress.... The second relevant community is the real flesh and blood community that will hopefully co-exist with its all-powerful neighbor." But usually, Simmons says, the community finds itself on the outside looking in when vital decisions are in the making.

For almost 100 years the citizens of the District were completely disenfranchised; not until the 23rd Amendment to the Constitution was ratified in 1961 could they even vote for president or vice president. Until 1973, Washington's last elected Mayor was Matthew Gault Emery in 1870. Then the Shepherd crisis brought about the territorial form of rule prevailing until Lyndon Johnson secured Congressional approval for a Commissioner (to be called Mayor) appointed by the president. Walter Washington became the first appointed black mayor of any major city in 1967. Six years later he was elected to that office after President Nixon signed the D.C. Home Rule Bill into law, permitting District residents to elect their mayor, council chairman and twelve other council members. Thus the apron strings were severed, but Congress still holds the purse strings. And 800,000 District taxpayers still have no Congressman; that many people in another area would be entitled to two Senators and two Representatives. Two hundred years ago a war was fought over the issue of taxation without representation.

Color has been another factor in the imbalance of power in Washington. A magazine article of 1940 reported that negroes who had lived in many parts of the country had found nowhere in America such mutual race hatred as in the capital. The District's City Council passed two ordinances barring racial discrimination during President Ulysses S. Grant's term, yet 78 years later Grant's grandson announced that the National Parks Commission would "arrange for the colored population dispossessed by new playgrounds, public buildings, parks and schools to be relocated in a remote section in the rear of Anacostia." This announcement was in line with the policy stated by a National Capital Housing Authority official of the effect that "Segregation is the accepted pattern of the Community."

Thus the government shapes not only the appearance of the city but the pattern of life of its residents. What is it like to live in the city some call "Uncle Sam's Company Town"?

For Jim Aldrich, a reporter who has spent a decade here as correspondent for the *New York Times*, it means working insane hours like four to midnight, with Mondays and Tuesdays off. It means belonging to a small army of more than 2,000 reporters, all competing to report the decisions made in the White House, Senate and House of Representatives, Federal Departments and the Supreme Court. For Jim the city is alive with memories of places and people, of beginnings and endings.

When he stands in the ornate caucus room on the third floor of the Senate Office Building, Jim remembers that it was here that John F. Kennedy announced his candidacy; then eight years later his brother Robert followed suit. And it was here also that another presidency began to end when a Senate Committe opened the Watergate investigation.

Jim recalls watching demonstrators protesting the War in Vietnam march down Pennsylvania Avene to the White House in 1970; they were turned back by buses parked nose-to-tail like wagon trains in a defensive circle in an old western movie. And he remembers rushing out of the White House on a spring night in 1975 with word that the last Americans had been evacuated from Saigon. He will never forget seeing Robert Kennedy hurrying across Capitol Plaza in 1968 on the way to a Senate roll call, with two other Senators needling him about whether he should run for president; then, a few months later, watching the tourists who waited patiently near the entrance to Memorial Bridge as the motorcade bearing Kennedy's body sped by, hours behind schedule, toward Arlington Cemetery.

Jim finds that power shifts quickly in Washington. The surprising thing is that it shifts without violence, although there are constant reminders of violence in Washington—workmen cleaning up the rubble from a bomb explosion in the Capitol Building in 1971; guards persuading a disgruntled citizen to surrender after he had crashed his car through a White House Gate one Christmas morning; Senator John Stennis limping onto the Senate floor after recovering from gunshot wounds in a robbery in front of his home in 1973.

Despite such incidents, there are no troops in the street when power passes from one person to another. August 9, 1974, for example, was a day of potential crisis; Jim and his associates were alert around the clock, watching developments closely, for no president had ever resigned before. But Richard M. Nixon said a tearful farewell to his staff and was on an airplane over Missouri when Gerald R. Ford was sworn in. Then after Ford failed in his bid for election, Jim called at the White House on Inauguration Day, 1977, to find aides and secretaries to Mr.

Ford wandering through the offices for the last time, and the staff of the new President looking at their new offices and trying to figure out the communication system.

Thus the people in power come and go like the tourists. Yet the historic buildings remain as symbols of something stronger, of a more permanent government. Jim feels that though it might not always be evident, the city really does belong to the people.

If you are young, well educated and moderately well off, Washington is "...a *nice* city—a fun place to live." That's how Laurie Rosen describes it, and she should know. She lives in the shadow of the Capitol dome on Duddington Place, in a 75-year old remodeled townhouse. Once known as a "railroad flat", it was built to house workers for the railroad a block away, who were mostly Italian or Irish. The old roundhouse south of Garfield Park is gone, but descendants of some of those workers still live on Duddington.

The owners take pride in painting the old brick townhouses in traditional colors with contrasting shutters and trim. No for-sale signs are in evidence; the location makes them in constant demand at around $50,000 before restoration. Only fifteen feet wide, they can be remarkably liveable.

Laurie has been married to Joel Rosen for eight years; she has a degree in law from Howard University, having previously spent three years as the only black student in her high school in Maryland, yet she denies ever having been subjected to racial prejudice. "Well, maybe once, when I was a child, but I thought it was funny. I went into a segregated restaurant and the manager said, "If she's fool enough to come in here, I'm fool enough to serve her."

Laurie was an attorney with the Office of the Public Defender until she resigned to start a family. Now she and Joel have Philip, six, Joseph, four, and Benjamin, nine months old. Plus an elegant female cat named Harry, and Ralph, a black Labrador with a head as big as a watermelon. Ralph never goes outside in the neighborhood except on a leash, but he does enjoy running in one of the three nearby parks. The Rosen's "backyard" is a wood deck four by eight feet.

Joel, too, has a degree in law (from Columbia University), but he works in construction. His business takes him into the oldest areas of the capital, where he buys run-down buildings and rehabilitates them into attractive offices, restaurants and apartments. He is enthusiastic about his job; he enjoys the contact with people, the challenge of making decisions in the field, and the fact that he usually works within five miles of home. The family attends Adas Israel Congregation, established in 1869.

Part of the joy of living on Duddington Place is the convenience of public transportation. Laurie takes the children everywhere, walking or on the bus—the National Zoo, the Smithsonian, the monuments. In spite of the District's much-talked about crime rate, Duddington has been free of incidents in their four-year residence there. "It's like a small town with one street a block long," Laurie says.

In spite of the Rosens' fondness for Duddington, they are looking for an new place to live. The transient nature of the younger residents, the increasing number of singles and childless-by-choice couples has prompted them to seek a neighborhood with more playmates for Philip, Joe and Ben. But they plan to keep the Duddington house, both as an investment and as a beloved old friend.

Letty Grove lives in the *other* Washington. Her brick rowhouse is almost the same age as the Rosens', but it has not been altered since its construction about the time of Letty's birth some seventy years ago. At $31 per month she expects to have it paid for in less than a year provided she can avoid refinancing it again as she has done twice in the past to meet overwhelming expenses.

Letty's grandmother was born into slavery in King George, Virginia, and emancipation made very little difference in the family's lifestyle. Letty and her six brothers and sisters worked beside their mother in the fields until Letty married and came to Washington in 1920. When her husband's early death left her with five children she worked on a W.P.A. project sewing uniforms for sanitation workers for ten years.

Now she shares her home with three grandchildren, Eben, 10, Paul, 15, and Cindee, 16, supporting them as a domestic worker. Her employers, the Keenes, pick her up at seven each morning and drive her twenty miles to their home in Chevy Chase. She works hard for $45 a week, cleaning and babysitting. She takes pride in her employer's neat, attractive home but she resents being told what to do, replying testily, "I can see what needs doing."

A niece, Roxanne, keeps an eye on the grandchildren after school. Letty is brusque with her grandchildren ; all day she has been gentle and affectionate with her employer's children and she is "used up". They eat pan bread, greens and milk and she sends them to bed early because she wants them off the streets. Cindee has been staying out late and Letty is concerned about her, and also about Eben's poor grades.

Letty admits to backaches and frequent bad headaches, but hasn't been to a doctor or dentist in thirty years; her smile exposes bare gums. She has never accepted either food stamps or welfare, but when her house is paid for she will quit her job and live on her Social Security.

Letty has never driven a car, nor ridden in a plane or train. She walks to a grocery store three blocks from home. Once a year she makes a complicated, expensive trip by bus to visit two sisters still living in King George, transferring four times each way.

She has never seen the memorial to the president who freed her grand-

24

mother, nor is she aware that the only monument ever erected on Federal land to a woman, and a black woman and daughter of a slave at that, is the statue of Mary McLeod Bethune in Emancipation Park, only blocks from her home. Letty might as well live in Scranton or Skidmore; the capital has no magic for her. But neither has King George.

There is no such thing as a typical Washingtonian. There is infinite variety in outlook, background, ambition and lifestyle. But if there is a thread that runs through the fabric of life for every District resident it is the feeling of impermanence. A fear—or just as often a hope—that tomorrow he or she will be somewhere else. Thousands come expecting to stay a year or two and linger for thirty or more. unwilling to give up the excitement, the power, the uniqueness of capital life. Others can't wait to leave the shadow of the Capitol and get back to the sunshine of their home town.

Suzanne West, a slim, quietly pretty redhead in her fifties, left a nine-room rambler in Springfield for a ninth-floor apartment near Mount Vernon Square following a traumatic divorce from her husband of 25 years. She found the consequences of the divorce more shocking than the death of her marriage—"like aftershocks of an earthquake," she says.

Her one-bedroom apartment is bright and spacious, but instead of a half-acre of grass and trees she tends a few potted plants. She hauls her laundry down nine floors to the basement "...as seldom as possible", and never leaves the building alone after dark. The clerk at the desk lets no one into the elevators without recognition. But in the daylight she walks to work at the National Archives, a vast store-house of Federal documents and drawings filed in steel cases and stored in catacombs deep inside the monumental building. Here she supervises one of three "Search Rooms", helping to process the 500,000 inquiries received each year. Of these about 10,000 are from persons seeking proof of age or citizenship.

The room in which she works is Italian Renaissance, with an elaborately painted cross-beam ceiling. Her friends invariably exclaim, "What a great place to work!" And it is. There is a relaxed, old-world atmosphere; her co-workers are friendly, and there are liberal insurance and retirement benefits plus free showings of motion pictures in the third-floor auditorium, but Suzanne sees the job as a dead-end, with mandatory retirement ten years in the future. The 1970 census reported 26,000 more women than men under 25 in Washington, and the proportion increases with age. So most of Suzanne's friends are women. Once she and a friend went to the Jefferson Memorial before work to see the cherry blossoms at their peak in the April sunshine, and she often takes a bag lunch to the Mall in order to enjoy the entertainment sponsored by the National Capital Parks Department.

There is no church in her immediate neighborhood, but Sunday often finds her hurrying to her former church in the suburbs, a forty-minute drive. She drives more slowly on the way back, savoring the green lawns and widely spaced homes, remembering...

But for those of us who live in those green, remote suburbs, the capital has an attraction like a flame to a moth, except that we know we'll get burned. We *know* traffic will be horrendous; parking places will be non-existent, and we'll probably get caught going the wrong way on a one-way street. But we also know that there is excitement waiting across the river that exists nowhere else in the country.

Every one-horse town has a Chinese restaurant; Washington has 41, with a choice of Cantonese, Szechuan, Peking or Mandarin. It also offers Afghan, Arabic, Caribbean, Cuban, Greek, Hawaiian, Irish, and four varieties of Indian food. There are Vietnamese, Indonesian and Thai restaurants, or Argentinian, Spanish, and Mexican if you prefer to dine in the Latin manner. Continental dining is available in 42 Italian places, and in 37 French restaurants at last count. Germany, Bavaria, Hungary, and Switzerland are all represented by several establishments. Vegetarian, health, and soul food are available, and the newest craze is the cafe-within-a-bookstore, where you can read while you eat, if you don't mind grease stains on the pages.

Nourishment for the mind is varied, too. There are ten major museums and uncounted minor ones, nine first-rate art galleries, and thirteen legitimate theaters. For rest and relaxation you can take your choice of 72 parks, circles, squares and playgrounds in the District.

But there are also delightful rewards to be found in the capital when least expected. Some of today's big society affairs and charity balls are being held at unlikely places such as Garfinckle's, the Old Post Office, Union Station, or the Botanical Gardens. You may run into a cabinet member while on the most mundane errand.

In Georgetown one day I rattled down M Street's cobblestones looking for a place to park and saw a policeman standing by a barricade at 31st Street. After turning left and going around the block only three times I found a parking space right on the corner. With my dime in the meter and my eye on my watch, I asked the policeman why the street was blocked.

"They're dedicating a statue of Justice Douglas," He jerked his thumb in the direction of the C & O Canal a half-block away. You couldn't see the canal for the people, all of them coming toward me carrying brochures. It was all over! Wanting to rescue the moment rather than let it slip away, I stopped the first man I saw.

"Excuse me, sir. Where did you get the brochure?"

The stranger, a small ruddy man in pin-striped suit, took my elbow. "I'm going to see to it that you get one. Let's go." He led me through the crowd. "Tell you what, let's go have a drink and maybe we can find one."

I drew back; he gripped my elbow tighter.

"No—this is a special party—I think I can get you in." And he propelled me up some steps, past a guard, to a long white table with cookies and green punch. And lots of brochures. I took two. He took a cup of punch.

He asked me where I was from and what I was doing. When I told him I was writing a book about Washington he lit up all over.

"Let me tell you my theory of what Washington will be like in the year 2,000. As an economist..." And he mentioned the World Bank, the International Monetary Fund and the fact that the Islamics had just purchased 100 acres near Dulles Airport. "Billions!" he said.

I couldn't bring myself to tell this economist with his billions that I was so worried about getting a two-dollar parking ticket that his fascinating theory was over my head.

"147 embassies in Washington now. All those ethnic restaurants—the Hong Kong of the Western World."

Then a guard motioned us aside and pushed a wheel chair bearing a frail man with translucent pale-pink skin and thin white hair through a doorway. Justice Douglas!

"And there's Warren Burger," Pinstriped suit nudged me. "They're *all* here." I felt dizzy. Was I really talking to a stranger from Massachusetts in a pin-striped suit, surrounded by Supreme Court Justices?

Then a woman walked up and said quietly, "That nice-looking young man over there"—she indicated with her eyes—"is Wendy's pediatrician."

That did it. I panicked. Hong Kong? Pediatrician? And who was Wendy? "Look, I told Pin Stripes, "My book won't be an in-depth study, and my car's parked in a metered space, and..."

"But let me tell you one more thing..." Baghdad on the Potomac. The Geneva of the Future. The Heartbeat of the World. Fascinated, I gave up. Even if the ticket cost fifteen dollars it would be worth it. So I heard how he came to Baghdad on the Potomac to prepare a paper for the president, and was offered not one but *two* positions and somehow lost both of them through political maneuvering.

"It's a jungle, Believe me," he said, "And let me tell you just one more thing..."

I started walking slowly toward my car while he told me how jobs are won or lost in the jungle. A pretty girl in a red dress went by and he lost his train of thought momentarily. "Uh...the most powerful nation in the world...a wonderful time to be living!"

We had reached my car at last, and I couldn't believe there was no ticket under my wiper. Well, what the heck! I put another nickel in the meter and got another hundred dollars' worth of information.

"Oh—'Tommy the Cork' was there—did you see him? He told me—now listen to this..."

The meter flag whirred and all I had left was a ten dollar bill. Fifteen minutes later we parted, having exchanged names and agreed that he would call me—"or maybe I'll put it in skywriting" if he received the appointment he wanted.

I'm still waiting for that message in the sky, but only in Washington, Hong Kong of the Western World, could I have rubbed shoulders with Tommy the Cork, all the Supreme Court Justices and Wendy's pediatrician for a total outlay of fifteen cents.

With all its richness and excitement today, tomorrow's Washington promises to be even more enticing, brighter than Baghdad, cleaner than Hong Kong. Every day brings rumors of new baubles of the Nation's jewel box—a National Aquarium, a planetarium, a three-square block convention center, a memorial to FDR, and even a bridge across the Channel to rival Italy's Ponte Vecchio, with three tiers of shops and restaurants.

Some of these dreams will never materialize, but changes are taking place as a result of the only major remodeling plan advanced for the District since 1920, the Owings Plan of 1964. Under the chairmanship of California Architect Nathaniel Owings, the commission emphasized three major areas of improvement for the Capital: the improvement of Pennsylvania Avenue, the creation of new facilities to add interest and enjoyment to Washington for both tourists and residents, and long-range planning for future growth of the city.

The Owings Plan's suggestion for growth planning has a science fiction touch—satellite cities spaced around the outer reaches of the Beltway, reached by high-speed elevated transit, with unused land set aside as permanent greenbelts between the corridors.... But Reston and Columbia, examples of successful satellite cities in Virginia and Maryland, grew in ten years from raw land to "New Towns" of 30,000 and 45,000 each; all they lack is the high-speed transportation, and that may be implemented when Metro reaches its full potential.

The Washington Metropolitan Transit System, or "Metro", the first in the country for mixed-mode travel (foot-bicycle-car-bus-train-plane), is in operation, with completion expected by 1984. $4\frac{1}{2}$ miles of the "Red Line" opened in 1976 with free rides for 51,200 people who waited in line for up to four hours; the "Blue Line" created similar excitement in 1977. When completed, there will be 101 miles of subway, with even the most distant stops,

Vienna and Springfield in Virginia and Rockville in Maryland, only a half-hour from Metro Center at 12th and G Streets.

Some of the proposals of the Owings Plan are already a part of the Washington scene—the Kennedy Center, the Martin Luther King Memorial Library, and the new reflecting pool and other improvements on the Mall.

The principal difference between Washington and other cities is that the Malls, museums and memorials of Washington belong to the people of the United States, and over 4,000,000 of them come every year to look at their treasures in Uncle Sam's safekeeping.

THE PLATES

THE CAPITOL

A competition offering a city lot and $500 for the best design for the U.S. Capitol in 1792 ended in a tie between French architect Stephen Hallet and William Thornton, a physician and amateur architect from England. The latter's plan was finally chosen and Hallett was hired to complete the working drawings and supervise construction. The cornerstone was laid in 1793 by George Washington in an elaborate Masonic ceremony, but jealousy and disagreements delayed the work until Benjamin Latrobe took over, completing the north and south wings joined by a 100-foot bridge, just in time for the British to burn them in 1814.

The original plans were saved, and Charles Bulfinch was hired to direct restoration of the two wings. He then added the central section, with a low dome over the rotunda. In 1851 new wings were added for the Senate and House of Representatives at a cost of nearly $8,000,000, giving the Capitol a total of 153,112 square feet of space. Then the old wooden dome looked too small, and it was replaced by an enormous cast iron dome with an estimated weight of almost 9,000,000 pounds.

The 36 columns surrounding the lower portion represent the 36 states in the Union at that time, and the 13 smaller columns encircling the 50-foot lantern symbolize the original thirteen states. Some say that it is fortunate that the statue of the Goddess of Liberty atop the dome is so far above the city, for it is a "mongrel" statue altered several times during its design. It has never been gilded because that would only emphasize its flaws. But under the 97-foot dome is a vast museum, and the frescoed ceiling of the rotunda took Constant Brumidi, an Italian immigrant, 25 years to paint.

THE NATIONAL VISITOR CENTER

Dangerous railroad crossings in Washington took the lives of some thirty persons each year before the new Union Terminal replaced three old depots in the city, including one on the Mall at Sixth and B Streets, in 1907. Designed by Daniel Burnham at a cost of $21 million including landscaping and statuary, it has a Central Pavilion with three enormous arches; on the cornice above are six 18-foot statues representing Fire, Electricity, Freedom, Inspiration, Agriculture and Mechanics. In front of the building is a semi-circular fountain featuring a 15-foot figure of Columbus.

By 1960 the airplane and automobile had cut sharply into railroad profits and the owners planned to demolish Union Station for construction of more profitable offices. It was saved for future generations when it was given landmark status in 1964. In 1968 the government purchased it for a National Visitor Center to be operated by the National Park Service.

There are information kiosks, a parking garage, services for the handicapped or foreign visitor, a National Bookstore, and two mini-theaters showing continuous films. A gallery of portraits of First Ladies and a collection of gifts presented to the Presidents and First Ladies are located in the 760-foot Concourse. In the lofty Main hall soaring 95 feet above street level is an award-winning eighty-screen slide show three stories high entitled "Welcome to Washington", with scenes of the city today and as far back as 1800, when visitors had a choice of arriving in the capital afoot or on horseback.

34

THE SUPREME COURT BUILDING

"Oyez! Oyez! Oyez! All persons having business before the Honorable, the Supreme Court of the United States, are admonished to draw near and give their attention, for the Court is now sitting. God save the United States and this Honorable Court."

From October to June of each year this century-old chant opens the session of the highest Court in the land in this classic white marble building at First and East Capitol Streets, N.E. Designed by Architect Cass Gilbert and completed in 1935, it is adjacent to the Library of Congress facing the Capitol.

When the first Supreme Court met in 1809 at Long's Tavern there were five associate justices and Chief Justice John Marshall. Today there are nine members who are appointed for life by the president subject to confirmation by the Senate. Their influence on the nation is so great that much care is taken in their selection; their social philosophy and moral character are considered as thoroughly as their legal knowledge and experience. Charles Evans Hughes, later a Chief Justice, said, "We are under a Constitution, but the Constitution is what the judges say it is."

About 2500 cases reach the Court each year, and one-sixteenth of that number are reviewed in detail. Decisions are made in secrecy on Fridays, and the majority decision is read in open court by its author. There are 144 seats available for the public from noon until 4:30. Nearly a half million visitors annually pass through the entrance portico, over which is carved "Equal Justice Under Law".

36

THE LIBRARY OF CONGRESS

Hundreds of gold-leafed rosettes gleam from the coffers of the dome over the Main Reading Room in the Library of Congress. The collar above bears twelve figures representing the countries that have contributed most to U.S. civilization. Around the lantern are eight windows topped with scalloped arches, and the ceiling of the lantern has a female figure representing "Human Understanding" attended by two cherubs against a painted sky. On the exterior the dome is surmounted by a gilded "Torch of Learning" 195 feet above the street. It appears that no portion of the building has been left unornamented. On the facade, 33 stone heads carved over the windows of the first story pavilions illustrate the facial characteristics of different ethnic groups.

Some hailed the florid Italian Renaissance building on First Street, S.E., as a masterpiece when it was completed in 1897, while others criticized it as an over-ornate "opera house". But the collection of books originally started for the use of Congress had overflowed the Capitol Building; some advocated lining the Capitol Dome with book-shelves, but Congress appropriated funds for the new building.

A copyright law of 1870 requires that two copies of every published work be deposited in the Library of Congress in order to obtain a copyright. Thus the institution houses sixty million pieces today, including books, periodicals, films, microfiches, and other records, plus museum items of inestimable value including a Stradivarius violin. There are dozens of specialized reading rooms, all heavily ornamented and decorated with major works of arts. Books are for reference only, and you must fill out a card requesting a specific volume; an aide will bring it to you if it is available.

An Annex completed in 1939 is almost Spartan in appearance next to the ornate main library, but is much more efficient, having been designed to hold ten million books in a smaller area than the original building.

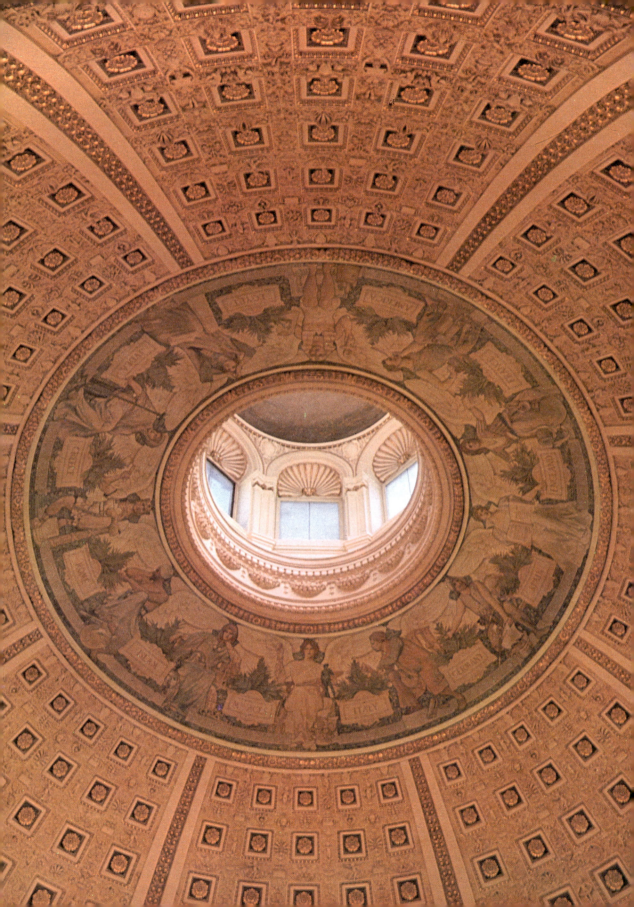

RIVER PARK HOMES

These innovative Washington homes have been much in demand since their
construction in 1962. Their convenient location, handsome contemporary
design, and the amenities offered have kept the vacancy factor at a very low 5%
average despite the fact that over 90,000 Washington families move each year.
The unusual arched windows and striking use of aluminum in the design were
planned by Architect Charles M. Goodman Associates for the developer, the
Reynolds Aluminum Corporation.

The 384 apartments offer a choice of efficiencies, one and two bedroom
apartment units, and there are 134 two-to-four bedroom town houses, all owned
by the residents on a cooperative basis, meaning they take an active part in the
management of their homes through the election of officers and frequent business
meetings open to all.

About one-fourth of the residents are government employees, including a
number of Congressmen who can walk the half-mile to the Capitol, and National
Airport is just across the river for visits to their constituencies. For families with
small children River Park has a cooperative nursery school with an enrollment of
twenty, and a swimming pool. The proximity of the Marina on the Potomac
River makes it easy for River Park boating enthusiasts to enjoy a sail or fishing
expedition after work or on the weekend.

40

WASHINGTON WATERFRONT

"Fresh fish! Come try my fish!" Fishmongers call out cheerfully to sightseers at Maine Avenue (formerly Water Street) east of 14th Street, S.W., a welcome change from the well-ordered government buildings of downtown Washington. Here are color, clutter and confusion on the Washington Channel, which opens into the Potomac River, through the Chesapeake Bay and thence into the Atlantic.

Fishing boats dock early in the morning to unload their redolent cargo or sell directly from their decks—oysters from Chincoteague or Tangier, bluefish and flounder from the Outer Banks, and sea trout from the mouth of the Potomac; blue crabs, softshell crabs, hardshell crabs, steamed crabs. . . .And there are fresh fruits and vegetables piled high in the stalls, with watermelons just off the boat from South Carolina looking like great clusters of fat green grapes. Eat 'em here or take 'em home! Or try one of the fine restaurants across from the wharves; some of them have tables on balconies overlooking the water.

At the foot of L and K streets is Pier 4. From here boats leave for cruises to Mount Vernon daily, with moonlight cruises offered during the summer. The District Harbor Police boats and the Fireboat are anchored at N Street, near the municipal pier built in 1941.

A century ago as many as 100 sailing vessels passed through the channel at a time. Today there are few large ships, but for small-craft enthusiasts rental slips are available near 14th Street at the end of the Channel. Moored near the Capital Yacht Club are sail boats with auxiliary engines and cabin cruisers that serve as year-round homes. Government employees and other District area workers find this an economical way to live, and one that enables them to enjoy cruising the Potomac after work on sultry summer evenings.

THE THOMAS JEFFERSON MEMORIAL

Thomas Jefferson requested that his monument should be a plain, three-foot cube surmounted by an obelisk six feet high. The design selected by the Memorial Commission, an adaptation of the Pantheon in Rome by John Russell Pope encountered violent criticism. Ultimately it was scaled down one-third and reduced in cost by one-half. Built primarily due to the efforts of Franklin Roosevelt, it was started in 1938 on land that was under water until filled in the late 1800's. The siting of the memorial across the Tidal Basin from the Mall necessitated removing some cherry trees. This enraged a group of ladies. who chained themselves to an uprooted tree. Later they learned that while 80 trees were removed for the project, there were already plans to add a thousand new ones on completion of the work.

The building is circular with four imposing colonnaded entrances facing the points of the compass, with a low dome similar to the design Jefferson used for the Rotunda of the University of Virginia. The interior features a 19-foot high statue of Jefferson in middle age. He wears knee-breeches and a full-length coat trimmed with furs given him by Thaddeus Kosciuszko, the Polish Engineer who directed construction of American fortifications during the Revolution. These furs had been a gift to Kosciuszko from Czar Paul I of Russia, and Jefferson wore the coat the rest of his life.

Surrounding the statue are four panels of famous Jefferson quotations, with a fifth inscribed at the base of the dome reading "I have sworn upon the Altar of God eternal hostility against every form of tyranny over the mind of man." This is particularly interesting in the light of the fact that Jefferson was an admitted agnostic.

44

THE WASHINGTON MONUMENT

The design chosen for the Washington Monument by competition in 1836 was an ornate Egyptian obelisk rising to 700 feet, with cornices and corbels, and a Greek temple encircling the bases. Fortunately, the project ran short of funds and it was simplified to a 555-foot tapered, unornamented shaft.

Construction began in 1848, financed by public subscription. A request for marble blocks in place of money brought over 250 stones from states, cities, foreign countries, churches, fraternal organizations, and even a fire station. Visitors are required to take the electric elevator to the top of the shaft (a $1\frac{1}{4}$ minute trip), but some choose to walk down the 898 steps in order to read the messages inscribed on these blocks.

When Pope Pius IX sent a stone from Rome in 1854 the radical American Party (or "know Nothings") stole the block, shocking the rest of the world. During the Civil War construction halted and for over twenty years the stub of the monument remained at a height of 150 feet. The grounds were used for cattle pens and slaughtering, causing pollution of the old Washington Canal, which had to be covered over. Congress finally appropriated funds to continue in 1876. A slight change in color at this point is due to the unavailability of the original marble after the long layoff.

Due to the thickness of the stone walls, which are 15 feet thick at the bottom tapering to 18 inches at the top, moisture condenses in the upper shaft resulting in a light rainfall sometimes requiring attendants to wear rain gear. Washington's most notable landmark, it is visited by some 2,000,000 visitors annually.

46

THE MALL LOOKING EAST

The Mall from 1830 to 1908 was the scene of chaos—sooty depots with coal or wood-fired trains chugging in and out while people and animals hurried to clear the tracks that ran north, south, east and west from the Capitol. The swampy land was often flooded by raw sewage in summer, and frozen in winter.

In 1871 Alexander "Boss" Shepherd asked the railroad to improve its roadbed at Maryland Avenue from First to Sixth Street, directly in front of the Capitol; tired of being ignored, he finally brought in 200 men from the Board of Public Works late one night and tore up the tracks before dawn broke. The McMillan plan brought about the new Union Station and the landscaping of the entire Mall area.

In this photo taken from the top of the Washington Monument the museums dominate the Mall. Along the left side are the Museum of History and Technology, Museum of Natural History and the National Gallery of Art with its new triangular Annex. On the right side, tucked into the trees, are the Freer Gallery, the Smithsonian Institution Headquarters, the Museum of Arts and Industries, the Hirshhorn Museum, and the new Air and Space Museum.

The colossal Ulysses S. Grant Memorial stretches 252 feet along First Street across the Capitol end of the Mall. It depicts General Grant on his favorite mount, Cincinnatus, with groups of Union Cavalry or infantry at each end of the granite base. The sculptor, Henry M. Shrady, was almost unknown when he was selected in 1902 to design the work but took extraordinary care in detailing the statues; he even joined the National Guard for four years to gain military experience. After many discouraging setbacks the Grant statue was placed on the base in 1920, the artillery and cavalry figures having been completed earlier. Shrady died of strain and overwork two weeks before the dedication in 1922.

48

THE MALL LOOKING NORTH

On L'Enfant's original plan the Mall was to end on a line drawn parallel to the White House grounds. Today it extends from the Potomac to the Capitol, with the White House and Ellipse at the side. In this view from the Washington Monument at the heart of the Mall, the Ellipse is in the foreground with a softball diamond and playground recommended by the McMillan Commission. Not visible but due south of the White House on the north border of the Ellipse is the Zero Milestone, a square stub of stone from which all distances from the Capital are computed.

The massive building on the left is the Executive Office Building, and on the right is the Treasury Department. The round pool in the center is part of the Boy Scouts Memorial unveiled in 1964. Beside the pool is a group of 12-foot high figures representing American Manhood and Womanhood, and a Boy Scout.

Behind the White House is 7-acre Lafayette Park, once a race course, then a market, and, during the War of 1812, an army encampment. In the center of the park is a statue of Andrew Jackson, the first "man of the people" elected to the presidency. At the four corners of Lafayette Park are statues of four generals from foreign countries who contributed to America's fight for independence. On the southeast corner General Lafayette is depicted standing in the French National Assembly seeking aid for Americans. On the southwest corner is another Frenchman, Major General Comte Jean de Rochambeau, commander of the 5500-man Royal French Expeditionary Force, which helped decide the outcome of the American Revolution.

On the northwest corner stands a bronze statue of General Frederick Wilhelm Von Steuben, a Prussian who spoke no English, but managed to train raw American recruits in a few weeks' time, called the most remarkable achievement in rapid military training in history. And on the north-east corner is Thaddeus Kosciuszko, Polish general who later returned to his native land to distinguish himself further in Poland's fight for freedom.

THE LINCOLN MEMORIAL

Daniel Chester French's 19-foot high statue of Abraham Lincoln seated in a chair facing the Capitol is probably the best-known statue in the world by an American artist. An estimated 100 million people have visited the memorial since its completion in 1922. Made from 28 perfectly fitted blocks of Georgian marble, it took four years to complete.

Efforts to erect a tribute to the much-loved president began soon after his assassination in 1865, but construction was delayed by controversy over the site, "...a God-forsaken, mosquito-stricken spot...", the design, "...an incongruous monument to a man of Lincoln's warmth and human kindness" and even the inscription over the statue. Now accepted to be the most eloquent in Washington, it reads, "In this Temple as in the hearts of the people for whom he saved the Union the memory of Abraham Lincoln is enshrined forever."

The site chosen was a swamp, and concrete pillars were sunk up to 60 feet deep in order to reach bedrock. Architect Henry Bacon was awarded the Gold Medal of the American Institute of Architects for the design of the Greek temple which houses the statues, after he had been carried by barge up the reflecting pool for the dedication ceremony.

The statue of the Emancipator is flanked by two of his finest contributions to American literature, cast in bronze. On the north wall is the Second Inaugural Address beneath a mural entitled "Reunion", symbolizing peace and progress following the Civil War. The south wall holds the Gettysburg Address and a mural representing "Emancipation", a fitting tribute to the president who declared, "If slavery is not wrong, then nothing is wrong."

IN THIS TEMPLE
AS IN THE HEARTS OF THE PEOPLE
FOR WHOM HE SAVED THE UNION
THE MEMORY OF ABRAHAM LINCOLN
IS ENSHRINED FOREVER

THE JOHN F. KENNEDY CENTER FOR THE PERFORMING ARTS

The red-carpeted Grand Foyer of the Kennedy Center is lit by eighteen Orrefors crystal chandeliers, the memorial gift of Sweden. Each is fifteen feet high and seven feet in diameter, containing 348 lights and 768 prisms, and totalling one ton in weight. The foyer is often the scene of special musical programs which are free to the public.

Originated as the National Cultural Center established by Congress in 1958, it became the official memorial to President Kennedy after his tragic death in 1963. Up to $15\frac{1}{2}$ million dollars in federal funds were allocated, to be matched by private donations. The final cost was nearly 70 million in spite of the many gifts from foreign countries, including all of the marble on both the exterior and interior, donated by Italy. Other gifts displayed throughout the Center are sculptures, tapestries, murals, paintings and silken curtains for the stages.

Three elegant theaters open off the foyer. Shown here is the stairway to the three-tiered Opera House, with 2,300 seats for viewing productions of ballet, modern dance, musical comedy and opera. The Eisenhower Theater, named for the late president and Mrs. Eisenhower, has 1,150 seats. Both contemporary and classic plays are presented here. The Concert Hall, with 2,750 seats, is home to the National Symphony, but also offers rock, folk, jazz, recitals and world-famous orchestras for all tastes.

The American Film Institute, a 224 seat movie theater, was an added afterthought tucked into the basement parking garage, but the Center makes an asset of it by decorating the cinderblock walls with automobile parts.

WATERGATE APARTMENTS

A household word now synonymous with infamy and intrigue, Watergate is actually a futuristic complex of three apartment buildings totalling 600 units plus nineteen opulent penthouses, a hotel and two office buildings. The break-in that precipitated the "Watergate Affair" took place in a suite of offices on the sixth floor of the office building at 2600 Virginia Avenue, N.W.

Watergate's location on Virginia Avenue across from the Kennedy Center is a major attraction, but for many Congressmen and other distinguished owners the principal benefits are probably the elegance and spaciousness of the apartments and the security provided by the door-man on 24-hour duty, plus a closed-circuit television camera surveying the lobbies, protecting residents from unwanted or unexpected visitors.

For the convenience of the residents and visitors alike there are exclusive shops and services as well as several restaurants. Also on the premises are indoor and outdoor pools, sauna and exercise rooms, and valet, maid and secretarial services.

Owned by Washington's political and social elite, Watergate Apartments sell for from $50,000 for an efficiency unit to $250,000 for the larger penthouses. Notable residents have included Jacob Javits, Russell Long, Robert Dole, Anna Chennault and Abraham Ribicoff. Watergate's 1977 tax assessment was $58,265,587, making it the most valuable piece of privately-owned real estate in the District of Columbia.

THE PAN AMERICAN HEALTH ORGANIZATION

Technicians monitoring a smoking, festering dump in Peru; a mid-wife hiking into the Ecuadorian highlands to help a woman give birth in a crude hut; a TB infected family in New Guinea receiving innoculations, and a gaucho in the pampas of Argentina lassoing a steer believed to have contracted hoof-and-mouth disease.

This sophisticated, ultra-modern building in Washington, D.C. seems far removed from these incidents, but it is the headquarters for the Pan American Health Organization, the regional agency for the World Health Organization, and from here teams are sent out to work in 29 countries. There are 150 full member states in **WHO**, divided into six regions—the African, American, Eastern Mediterranean, European, Southeast Asian and the Western Pacific.

In the area long known as "Foggy Bottom", the headquarters on Virginia Avenue near E Street was designed by Uruguayan architect Roman Fresnedo Siri. The circular building contains the Council Chambers, and the ten-story curved tower holds offices for the staff. Fountains splash and sparkle in the entrance plaza, symbolizing life, health and abundance in keeping with the organization's purpose, "...the promotion and coordination of hemispheric efforts to combat disease, lengthen life, and promote physical and mental health."

Swifter-than-sound flight has made the world our neighborhood; what threatens the outermost island of New Guinea also threatens us. PAHO teams eradicated yellow fever in the thirties; in the seventies their targets are water, soil and air pollution, heart disease and cancer, and high infant mortality.

58

THE PAN AMERICAN UNION BUILDING

Washington, D.C., was the site of the first conference of the International Union of American Republics, later renamed the Pan American Union, in 1890. Now termed the General Secretariat of the Organization of the American States, or OAS, the headquarters is this handsome white marble building erected in 1908 at a cost of $1,100,000, largely a gift of Andrew Carnegie.

This view shows the rear of the building, with the reflecting pool and gardens where concerts featuring Latin American music are given in summer by the United Service Orchestra. The main entrance on 17th Street near Constitution Avenue, across from the Ellipse, has three arched doorways with a group of statuary by Gutzon Borglum symbolizing North America, and a second group by Isidor Konto representing South America. Above are carved panels depicting Washington's farewell to his generals, and Simon Bolivar's meeting with San Martin.

The barrel-vaulted ceiling of the marble entrance hall rises two full stories, and the interior skylit patio is a tropical garden with colorful macaws and a pink marble fountain. The Hall of the Americas, an impressive room 100 feet long by 70 feet wide on the second floor, is used for inter-American conferences and has stained glass windows and enormous chandeliers of crystal. But the main feature of this room is the display of flags representing the twenty-four countries participating in the OAS.

When expansion of the OAS required added office space a three story building was erected in 1946 at 19th and Constitution, with a 480-foot tunnel connecting the two buildings. A total of 1,000 persons are now employed by the regional headquarters. The purposes of the OAS include promoting the security, protection, cultural and economic development of the hemisphere.

60

OCTAGON HOUSE

Legends about suicides , mysterious bells that ring at odd hours of the night, and of wailing ghosts of cruelly treated slaves who come back to haunt their masters have made Octagon House the best-known haunted mansion in the capital.

Not an octagon at all, this unusual house has six sides including the curved entrance wall, and a novel shape with queer angles in the side and back to make optimum use of the acute angle formed at New York Avenue and Eighteenth Street, just two blocks from the White House.

The entrance hall is twenty feet in diameter, with two cast-iron wood stoves set in niches. An arched doorway leads into the stair-hall, where oval loops of stairs rise three stories; it is from this height that a young lady is said to have thrown herself to her death after a thwarted love affair.

Designed in 1800 by Dr. William Thornton for a wealthy Virginia planter, Colonel John Tayloe, it was occupied by President and Mrs. James Madison after the British burned the White House in 1814. The Treaty of Ghent ending the War of 1812 was signed in a front room on the second floor in 1815. Dolley Madison entertained many distinguished visitors here, including Lafayette and Von Steuben, as well as Jefferson, Monroe and John Quincy Adams.

During the Civil War, Octagon House served as a military hospital and later as a school. In 1902 it became headquarters for the American Institute of Architects until they constructed their own enormous building that curves around the Octagon like an elephant trying to cozy up to a rabbit. Today it is a museum; renovation revealed that the mysterious bells could have been due to rats chewing on the old-fashioned bellwires.

THE EXECUTIVE OFFICE BUILDING

Variously termed "baroque", "French Second Empire", and an architectural infant asylum", the Executive Office Building originally housed the State, War and Navy Departments. Connected to the White House by the latter's West Terrace, it now contains the office of the Vice President and a number of miscellaneous departments including the Bureau of the Budget and the National Aeronautics and Space Council.

The gray granite structure cost nearly $10,500,000 in 1888, and has three main floors, with a six-story pavilion in the center of each facade. Its 900 small, unornamented columns, mansard roof with sharp dormers and tall chimneys topped with over-size chimneypots give it a whimsical, old-Europe appearance.

The interior has two miles of corridors, four circular stairways, and two fancifully decorated libraries. The Pennsylvania Avenue entrance has on its walls bronze plaques bearing the names of State Department officials who lost their lives in the line of duty, with the cause of death. The first entry reads, "William Palfrey, lost at sea, 1780." Another plaque honors the 240,000 horses and mules used in World War I.

The monument directly in front of the building is the First Division Memorial, a 15-foot gilt Winged Victory on a 60-foot column erected in 1924 to honor the valor of the Army's First Division.

64

THE WHITE HOUSE

The most prestigious address in the United States is 1600 Pennsylvania Ave, Washington, D.C. On 18 acres of land reclaimed from a swamp, the White House was eight years in construction and has been in a constant state of change ever since. Thomas Jefferson added colonnaded wings to provide space for offices, stables, a meat house, ice house and storage rooms for wine, coal and wood. The North Portico, shown here, was built in Andrew Jackson's era. This statue of Jackson is in Lafayette Park north of the White House. During his two terms over $50,000 was spent on refurbishing. In 1949 a five million dollar reconstruction was required because the foundations were on the verge of collapse.

Largest of the public rooms in the White House is the 87-foot East Room, decorated in white and gold, with three elaborate gold chandeliers and very old portraits of Martha and George Washington. The latter painting was rescued by Dolley Madison just before the British put the torch to the White House in 1814. In this elegant room, Theodore Roosevelt staged a Chinese wrestling match and later a contest between an American wrestler and a Japanese jujitsu artist.

Then there is the State Dining Room, capable of seating 140 guests, the oval-shaped Blue Room, and various other rooms used as reception areas or to display priceless relics of past administrations. The second and third floors are open only to the first family, guests and staff.

66

CONSTITUTION AVENUE

Looking west on Constitution Avenue from Twelfth Street, on the right you
see the entrance portico to the Departmental Auditorium adjoining the Labor
Department on the east and the Interstate Commerce Department on the
west, all a part of the gargantuan Federal Triangle. Across the street is a
portion of the Smithsonian Institution's Museum of History and Technology,
erected in 1964. There are three floors of exhibits; if you enter from Constitution Avenue you'll be on the first floor, crammed with cars and clocks, locks
and locomotives, harvesters and hayrakes. On the second floor, entered from
the Mall, you can't miss the 32-foot long original Star Spangled Banner, the
stellar exhibit of a whole floor of historical gems.

Did you ever wonder who selects the design of government buildings
such as those of the Federal Triangle? It is done by a committee, naturally.
A nine-member panel of architects and engineers rates the credentials of
interested designers, and the 3-member staff of the Public Building Service
interviews the top five candidates and recommends one. The head of General
Services Administration makes the final decision.

Ada L. Huxtable, critic and writer for *Progressive Architecture*, says
"Washington still waits for its 20th Century monuments. It can't hide behind
those beautiful trees forever."

THE SMITHSONIAN INSTITUTION

An eccentric British chemist in 1838 left a legacy to the United States of 105 bags containing over 100,000 gold sovereigns for the founding of an institution to increase and diffuse man's knowledge. Congress debated for years before deciding to accept James Smithson's bequest, and then created a Board of Regents to administer the fund. At that time the Board included the President of the United States, but today it is composed of the Vice President, the Chief Justice, three Senators, three members of the House of Representatives, and nine citizens from various geographical areas.

The original building, this "Castle on the Mall", of red sandstone, was designed by James Renwick, Jr. It was built between 1847 and 1855, and has nine towers, six of them primarily decorative. During the Civil War Abraham Lincoln watched Army Signal Corpsmen practicing with lanterns from the main tower.

For thirty years the "Castle" housed all the activities of the Institution, but today it serves as headquarters for the coalition of bureaus that have evolved. Many people are not aware of the scope of the Smithsonian, which has a catalogued inventory of more than 70 million objects, and operates the National Museums of Natural History, Air and Space, and History and Technology, six major art galleries, the National Zoo and the Kennedy Center. It also participates in many other programs in cooperation with universities, government agencies and institutions throughout the world, having shared in over 2,000 scientific expeditions. Affectionately dubbed "the nation's attic", the Smithsonian is no fusty old relic, but a vital part of today's technology.

70

PETERSEN HOUSE

"The House Where Lincoln Died" was owned by a tailor, William Petersen, who had his shop in the basement and rented rooms to soldiers and government employees. It is directly across from Ford's Theater on Tenth Street where Lincoln was shot by actor John Wilkes Booth on April 14, 1865.

Doctors who examined the President's wound realized he could not survive, and rather than subject him to a rough ride across cobblestone streets to the White House, ordered him carried to the boarding house across the street and laid diagonally across the too-short bed of a government clerk. Mrs. Lincoln waited in the front parlor, and it is said that every prominent person in Washington passed through the house that night. When Lincoln died early the next morning, Secretary of War Edwin M. Stanton, who interviewed witnesses to the shooting, declared, "Now he belongs to the ages."

The government purchased the house in 1896 as a National Shrine, and five patriotic women's organizations under the direction of U.S. Grant III restored and furnished it. Visitors walk up curved steps to the entrance and through a dark hallway to a small, sparsely furnished bedroom at the rear. The bed is a copy of the original, but the pillow is the very one on which Lincoln lay dying.

Ford's Theater closed immediately after the tragedy, and was converted to government offices. In 1893 the interior collapsed, killing 22 and injuring 68. Later it was used as a museum, until Congress voted 2.7 million dollars to completely reconstruct it. Now open to the public for tours, it is again used as a theater for showing-musicals, one-man shows and family plays. The basement of the theater houses the Museum of Lincoln Memorabilia, with 3,000 pieces including Booth's spur that caught in the flag on Lincoln's box, causing the assassin to fall and break his leg.

72

THE NATIONAL GALLERY OF ART

At Sixth and Constitution Avenue where the ugly old Pennsylvania Railroad depot once stood until eliminated by the McMillan Commission, the 785-foot long National Gallery is the largest marble structure in the world. Designed by J.R. Pope in a style somewhere between Roman and Greek, the $15,000,000 building is expected to stand for 1,000 years. Started with a nucleus of 120 paintings owned by Andrew Mellon, Secretary of the Treasury from 1921 to 1936, it is becoming one of the finest collections in the world with over 27,000 paintings, sculptures and art objects. The windowless building is lighted by laminated glass in the ceilings by day, and by concealed floodlamps at night, said to be among the finest lighting systems in the world. Elaborate air conditioning maintains even temperature and humidity to protect the priceless paintings.

The main entry hall is a rotunda one hundred feet in diameter with a 100-foot high dome supported by 24 green marble columns. There are 100 exhibition rooms on this floor, each decorated in a style reminiscent of the period or country of the paintings displayed. The visitor can start at the earliest period and move on, century by century, to the modern artists.

Mellon's son, Paul, and daughter Ailsa are expanding the gallery with the National Gallery of Art *East* Building at Madison and Pennsylvania Avenue. Sleekly modern, it will be in the form of two triangles with a connecting link containing new restaurant facilities. The small triangle will provide space for advanced study in the visual arts, and the larger for an exhibition gallery.

THE BRITISH EMBASSY

Americans calling the British Embassy Office in mid-June may be surprised to hear that the offices are closed due to the Holiday. A holiday in *June*? For the bit of England that is the British Embassy at 3100 Massachusetts Avenue, it is indeed a holiday. Each year the British Ambassador invites about 3,000 distinguished guests to celebrate the Queen's Birthday, not on her birthday, April 21, but in June when the weather is at its best and the Embassy gardens are in full bloom.

Strawberries and rich cream are the traditional fare, and invitations are craved by Anglophiles of the area, who wear their best garden-party finery for the occasion. For many years invitations to affairs at the British Embassy have been considered second only to those from the White House because the Queen Anne-style red-brick and white stone Embassy is the most magnificent in Washington. Built in 1931 on six acres at a cost of $1,000,000, the three story structure with a steep roof and towering chimneys is surrounded by terraces and gardens. Adjoining the Embassy is the newer (1960) British Chancery, a functional marble building with a copper-covered dome and glass walls that cost more than $3,000,000.

The Chancery has a staff of over 500 persons whose duties include issuing travel visas, attending to the needs of British citizens here, gathering and transmitting information helpful to diplomacy, trade and commerce, and promoting Britain in general.

On a hillside between the garden and the street is a statue of Winston Churchill. The site was chosen so that the former Prime Minister could have one foot on English soil of the Embassy and the other on American soil. The bronze statue is nine feet high, and Mr. Churchill's righ hand is raised in the "V for Victory" sign; in his left is his omnipresent cigar.

76

THE NETHERLANDS EMBASSY

Although the elegant residence of the Netherlands Ambassador to the United States on S Street is not the newest or largest of the 147 along Embassy Row, it is one of the best-arranged and most comfortable according to its present occupant. Built in 1929 by Wilmer Bolling, a brother of the second Mrs. Woodrow Wilson, for the Owsley family, it was purchased after World War II by the Dutch Government.

The large entrance foyer has a pair of graceful, curved starways leading to the reception rooms on the second floor, which can accomodate 800 people. A splendid crystal chandelier hangs over the dining room table, which seats 32 guests when fully extended; for larger parties up to six tables for ten each can be set up. Both rooms are decorated in soft, delicate pastels to set off the very beautiful, centuries-old tapestries and paintings by noted Dutch artists.

A charming, informal library opens onto a stone terrace shaded by magnolias, with herbs looking very much at home tucked in-between rose bushes by the embassy's maid.

In March of each year nearly 1700 blossoms of many colors and varieties are flown in by KLM for the Tulip Reception. Lavish bouquets are arranged throughout the home, and invited guests are distinguished diplomats, government officials and members of Washington Society. Later in the spring, red and yellow tulips bloom in profusion in front of the embassy for the pleasure of all passersby.

THE PIERCE MILL

Located in 1,800-acre Rock Creek Park, Pierce Mill dates from 1822 when millwright Isaac Pierce owned extensive property here and built a house, a distillery, spring house, sawmill and barns as well. The three-story and attic millhouse has an undershot wheel (meaning that it is turned by water running underneath the wheel) that operates three pairs of $4\frac{1}{2}$ foot millstones, two of them part of the original setup.

The miller and his helper could process about seventy bushels of corn, wheat, buckwheat or rye a day, keeping a one-eighth share for payment. Presumably it was this grain that he used to manufacture spirits in his distillery nearby.

To keep the millstones sharp a stonedresser came once a week to chip and roughen the surfaces. Operated by hired millers for nearly 75 years until the main shaft broke in 1897, it served as a teahouse during the depression. In 1936 it was reconstructed by the Public Works Administration and today Pierce Mill grinds flour for visitors, a living demonstration of the old techniques.

Other facilities located in Rock Creek Park are the National Zoo, the Rock Creek Nature Center with its exhibition hall, auditorium and planetarium, and the Joaquin Miller Cabin where the California poet lived around 1885; it was moved to the site from its original location on 16th Street by the California State Society.

THE NATIONAL PRESBYTERIAN CHURCH

Flags from 72 countries are displayed in the narthex of the National Presbyterian Church on Nebraska Avenue, N.W., representing the nations participating in the World Alliance of Reformed Churches. Presently performing dual functions, the church serves both as a local parish church and as an agency of the General Assembly of the United Presbyterian Church.

This modern church can trace its roots back to 1792 when George Washington laid the cornerstone for the White House. Some of the Scottish stone-masons who worked on the construction of the Executive Mansion began holding simple services in a carpenter's shed on the grounds. Later the group met in private homes, in a Masonic lodge, and even in the basement of the unfinished Capitol Building until the congregation built the "Little White Church Under the Hill" on the south side of Capitol Hill in 1812. The church was spared by the British when they destroyed most of the capital two years later, and the congregation continued to grow. A large brick church was erected on $4\frac{1}{2}$ Street (sic) N.W.; over the years its worshippers included Andrew Jackson, James Polk, Franklin Pierce, James Buchanan, Ulysses Grant, Grover Cleveland and many congressmen and justices. When the location was taken over for contruction of government buildings the congregation merged with that of the Church of the Coventry in 1930.

A suitable site for the construction of a National Church was found in 1966 at the former Hillcrest Children's Center across from American University. President Dwight D. Eisenhower laid the cornerstone in 1969. Existing buildings were utilized for residences, classrooms and offices, and a new building was designed by Harold Wagoner providing administrative facilities and a sanctuary featuring 42 semi-abstract stained glass windows. A 173-foot tower has been a landmark since its erection as part of the complex; appropriately for this electronic age, the bells that are heard chiming every half-hour and playing favorite hymns such as *Faith of Our Fathers* at noon and six daily are taped and electronically amplified.

82

THE NATIONAL CATHEDRAL

A moon rock brought back by the U.S. Astronauts in 1969 has been placed in the Space Window of the 14th century gothic National Cathedral. Designed by Rodney Winfield of St. Louis, the window illustrates the use of modern symbolism liberally combined with the traditional in the edifice.

Also known as the Cathedral of Saints Peter and Paul, it is the seat of the Protestant Episcopal Diocese of Washington but has no membership of its own, and receives no support from the Episcopal Church. Open to all, it fulfills the concept of a "House of Prayer for all People" first advanced by Pierre L'Enfant.

Established in 1907 on a 58-acre site on Mt Alban, it is laid out in the form of a cross 525 feet long by 275 feet wide. The 300-foot main tower, "Gloria in Excelsis", shown, contains a 53-bell carillon and a peal of ten bells for the ancient ritual of "change ringing". The gilded bronze statue in the foreground is titled "Lieutenant General George Washington on Horseback."

Fascinating carvings of limestone are found in unexpected places. On the flying buttresses are carved animals or demons with large noses from which water can drip to the roof below, and gargoyles expel rainwater from the gutters through their mouths. The 104-foot high nave was completed in time for the nation's Bicentennial celebration with the installation of the last of three large rose windows, the West Rose by Rowan LeCompte, designer of over twenty of the Cathedral's exquisite stained glass windows. A special guest for the nave's dedication on July 8, 1976, was Queen Elizabeth II.

Now about two-thirds complete, construction is expected to continue for decades. When finished it will rival Europe's finest medieval cathedrals.

84

DUMBARTON OAKS

Not a place for a casual outing for a family with small children, Dumbarton Oaks is a center for scholars and serious students of Byzantine, Medieval and Pre-Columbian history and art.

Built in 1801 by Judge William Dorsey, the house had changed hands many times and was in poor condition when purchased by Ambassador to Argentina and Mrs. Robert Bliss in 1920 to house their extensive collection of Byzantine and related art. The home was extensively remodeled and the grounds carefully landscaped in an effort to produce a formal garden equal to the finest in Europe. Shown here is the Pebble Garden, made of pebble mosaics, which is covered by a 2-inch film of water in spring and summer. The fountain at the end holds sculptures dating from around 1800 of three seahorses ridden by cherubs.

In 1933 the estate was formally established as the Dumbarton Oaks Center for Byzantine Studies. Primary emphasis is on the period beginning with the founding of Constantinople in 326 until the capture of the city in 1453 by the Turks. Related areas also covered are Hellenic, Medieval and Pre-Columbian research, including history, literature, law, music, and archaeology. The Center was transferred to Harvard University in 1940.

The Research Library today contains 75,000 bound volumes, 38,000 photographs, 7,500 slides plus thousands of microfiches. The Garden Library specializes in books and manuscripts relating to landscape architecture dating back over 400 years.

A modern glass, marble and brass addition designed by architect Philip Johnson was built in 1963 to house the Pre-Columbian Collection. The contrast between the eight circular glass pavilions grouped around an atrium with fountains and greenery in this wing and the formal brick architecture of the older building emphasizes the antiquity of the tapestries, jewelry, ceramics and mosaics crafted as early as 1200 B.C.

THE OLD STONE HOUSE

Tucked into the eclectic shops on busy M Street in Georgetown, the Old Stone House is probably the oldest home in the District of Columbia. Cabinet maker Christopher Layman built it in 1765 on Parcel No. 3 of the original 80 lots of Georgetown, and operated his shop on the ground floor until his death that same year.

Cassandra Chew, a prosperous business woman, used it for a combination home and ordinary (a colonial term for restaurant), and it later passed into her daughter's ownership. For a century the historical significance of the property was ignored; it served as a used car lot when Georgetown residents petitioned Congress to purchase and restore it in 1950.

Today the National Park Service administers the building, and costumed attendants guide the public through the narrow halls and modest rooms. They also cook their meals in the fireplace. We found a stew bubbling in a fat black pot over a smouldering fire. "Wet wood doesn't make a good cook fire," the attendant said ruefully. "I'm afraid our stew is watery and the meat a little chewy."

Upstairs in the dormered bedroom a spinning wheel and loom look as if the weaver had just stepped out the door for a moment, but a strange looking contraption made of wood baffles even the veteran tourist. The guide reveals it is a quilling box, used to shrink homespun thread or rag strips for making rugs.

GEORGETOWN HOUSES

In 1791 George Washington pronounced Georgetown "the greatest tobacco market in the state, if not the Union." When the Federal Government moved to Washington nine years later the newcomers were dependent on Georgetown, which had been in existence for 100 years, for housing.

The architectural distinction and beauty of Georgetown is mainly in the homes constructed during the early 1800's. Dr. William Thornton, designer of the original Capitol Building and a close friend of George Washington, is thought to have been the creator of the Federal style prevalent in Georgetown at that time.

Brick was the natural material for homes because the soil of the area was red or salmon-colored clay, ideal for molding into bricks. Claypits were often dug near the construction site, and kilns set up for baking the bricks, which were also used for sidewalks, gutters, and even streets.

Federal architecture is noted for its restraint and delicacy of scale. Georgetown had an area of only about one square mile; lots were small, and houses were usually built close to the street, with a walled garden in the rear. Steps leading to the entry often had delicate wrought iron handrails. Doorways had circular or elliptical heads, often with fan-lights. The entrance and hall were generally at the side, with the stairway and several rooms opening from the hall. Interiors were plain, usually plastered from ceiling to baseboard. Floors were of wide pine planking, oiled and polished. Typical dormer windows had circular-head sash. Shutters and entrance doors were almost invariably dark green, with other wood trim painted white.

Today Georgetown is one of the capital's most desirable areas, with narrow townhouses similar to these selling for as much as $115,000 if restored.

GEORGETOWN UNIVERSITY

In 1879, the year Washington was founded, Father John Carroll opened the first Catholic Institution of higher learning in the United States. Father John was a friend of George Washington and Benjamin Franklin, and a cousin of Charles Carroll, a signer of the Declaration of Independence. In accordance with the principles of that document, Father John decreed that the school should be open to "students of every religious profession."

The first school building at Georgetown University, Old South, was torn down to make way for new construction, but the second one, Old North, still stands. Opened in 1791, lack of funds delayed its completion until 1805 when the school's president, faculty and students worked together to finish it. It was in Old North that George Washington addressed the students when he visited his grand-nephews, Bushrod and Augustine Washington.

It appears that no attempt has been made to follow a particular style of architecture over the years, and the result is an uninhibited conglomeration of 55 buildings, each with a personality all its own. The photo shows the ultra-modern Lauinger Library, with its Romantic Classic neighbor, Maguire Hall, built in 1854.

With an enrollment approaching 12,000, the 102-acre campus provides housing for 3200 students; there are 10 schools administered by Georgetown, including the Law Center at 800 New Jersey Avenue in downtown Washington. The School of Medicine, established in 1850, is the second largest in the nation; it has thirteen buildings, including the 379-bed University Hospital which treats almost 21,000 patients yearly in its emergency room alone.

Georgetown's School of Foreign Service was the first in the U.S. and is the largest in the world. The university also offers Study-Abroad programs in England, Europe, the Middle East, Latin America and Japan. Its students staff embassies and diplomatic posts throughout the world.

FRANCISCAN MONASTERY

Carvings, paintings, stained glass, sculpture and rich mosaics present a capsulated impression of some of the most notable art of the Christian world at the Franciscan Monastery in northwest Washington. Erected in 1899 on Mt. St. Sepulchre, a wooded hilltop in Brookland, this was the first Franciscan Community in the United States, Financed by the sale of paper bricks, it was almost debt-free when completed.

The magnificent Byzantine Church features eighteen reproductions of shrines, altars and chapels of the Holy Land, and beneath the church is a reproduction of the Catacombs of Rome. Tucked into the hillside is an accurate copy of the Chapel at Lourdes, France.

The architect was Aristides Lonori of Rome, who visited the Holy Land to measure and photograph the places to be reproduced. He designed a colonnaded portico surrounding the church, with fifteen chapels. The landscaped gardens have statues of St. Francis, St. Christopher and Fr. Godfrey Shilling, O.F.M., Founder of the church.

Behind the church is the Monastery, with living quarters for the Friars, a library, infirmary and chapel. Also known as the Commissariat of the Holy Land for the United States, the Monastery has sent more than sixty-five friars to the Holy Land, where they have worked to restore and preserve ancient sites of importance to the Christian world, and provided schools, hospitals, orphanages, and churches there.

94